Presentation

Dear ....

Our times of trial and testing are but an invitation to lean heavily upon One who understands and cares. May the message of this book bring you into true relationship with the God who gives deliverance through suffering. You'll find His patience and strength sufficient, whatever the circumstance.

Sincerely yours,

____

by

NORMAN B. HARRISON, D.D.

"HE GIVETH MORE GRACE"

HIS INTERNATIONAL SERVICE
Minneapolis, Minn. 55423

CONTENTS

What Does It Mean?
I Peter 4:12, 19

"It does not matter what it means, poor heart;
The dear Lord knows, to bear it is your part;
Nor think some strange thing happens unto you
Which He would not allow so if He knew.
He does know. In His all-wise Fatherhood
He knows it, and allows it for your good.
He is not hard; you do not think He is
When in the dark you find your hand in His;
When it was light you tried to walk alone,
And thought the strength He gave you all your own.
You did not ask what that last blessing meant;
Just smiled and took it, satisfied, content.
You did not think it strange. You thought He knew,
And planned the sweet surprise which came to you.
Tried one, then do you take life's sweet and good,
Yet cannot trust that tender Fatherhood,
But think it makes mistakes whene'er it sends
Some hindrance which your eager haste offends?
Or when He lets the wicked plot you harm,
And stir a whirlwind when you seek a calm:
You think it strange, this trial swift and keen,
And in your weakness ask, "What does it mean?"
I think the language of God's heart would read,
'I love My child, I note his slightest need;
I long to prosper him in all his ways,
To give him quiet nights and peaceful days,
But if I do, he'll lose himself from Me,
My outstretched hand he will not wait to see;
I'll place a hindering wall before his feet;
There he will wait and there we two will meet.
I do it not in wrath for broken laws
Or willful disobedience, but because
I want him nearer, and I cannot wait
For him to come for he might wander late.
My child will wonder, will not understand,
Still half in doubt he'll clasp My outstretched hand;
But when at last upon My heart he leans
He will have ceased to wonder what it means.' "

I

SUFFERING — A Mystery

"Man is born unto trouble"—Job 5:7.

We live in a world of Suffering. It is not merely global; it is universal. Is this common lot of man accidental? or is it even incidental?

God suffered first. He has suffered excruciatingly. He suffers still. Could God not have avoided suffering for Himself? Could He not in turn have spared man these millenniums of suffering?

If He could have and did not, if He can now and does not, is not God's goodness called into question?

If God did not shrink from Suffering, but gave Himself to it, should man on his part seek to escape it? So doing, would he miss something of real value to himself?

Is Suffering inseparable from the system of evil? or are we to find in it that which makes for our good?

These are a few of the questions that crowd into the mind in the face of the Mystery of Suffering. Why is life—God's life, man's life, animal life, plant life—such as it is, subject to struggle, to pain and injury? Why is it constantly caught in the meshes of

Suffering? The right answer to these questions will bring one into the sanctuary of understanding where the dark mystery of existence is resolved.

"Man that is born of woman is of few days, and full of trouble" (Job 14:1). His life begins with travail by his mother; it ends in a wail of lament by his friends. With such boundaries what lies between?

He has eyes to see. These eyes are dimmed, shutting out the sun and the beauties of nature; he gropes his way. He has ears to hear. They become stopped; he is a prisoner whom the voices of friends and the strains of music cannot reach. He has hands to work. They palsy, limp at his side; his career is ended. He has feet to walk. They are crippled by disease or accident; he sits helplessly set aside. He has lungs to breathe, until germs riddle them; a stomach for nourishment, until some malady appears; a brain to think, until it fails him and he becomes one more of the thousands of "inmates."

In all these fields man's multiplied sufferings have created "specialists"—thousands of specialists giving themselves through long hours to the work of relief. Then there is the vast throng of sufferers for whom no relief ever comes; they just go on suffering.

Still greater is the agony of mental anguish. Fond hopes dashed to the ground; life plans hopelessly wrecked; bosom friends betraying; a reputation ruthlessly assailed; a partner ruining one's business; a life's companion found disloyal; a beloved son or daughter bringing sad disgrace. Then, perchance, remorse for evil deeds or fatal mistakes gnawing day and night at one's vitals—that haunting word, "remember!"

Any of these, singly or in combination, may so afflict one as to assail the reason with benumbing questions: Is there a God? Does He care? Is there no relief? Why is life a prolonged struggle? A vale of tears? Why this dark mystery of suffering?

Job Has the Answer

Job's experiences, taken by themselves, merely disclose the mystery—altogether too deep for his friends to fathom. But the book of Job is placed in our hands as the divine key to resolving the mystery.

Job was a good man and godly. God owned him as "My servant Job—none like him—perfect—upright" (Job 1:8; 2:3). But in one stroke he was stripped of his possessions; then of his family; then in the place of personal health, comfort and esteem came disease, distress and loathesomeness.

Job's three friends reasoned that such suffering indicated sinfulness that must be confessed. This is the best the philosophy of worldly wisdom could suggest. But it drove Job to self-justification, defeating the very purpose of his sufferings. So the book is given to us, its purpose being to take us behind the scenes. We are permitted to see—

1—The Hand of Satan. Satan has accused God of bribing Job to be good—of buying his loyalty with wealth and health. Remove these and "he will curse Thee to Thy face," said Satan (Job 1:9-12; 2:4-8). Could that possibly be? (with Job or with you?). God's honor is at stake. By God's permission Job's sufferings follow. They are a test. They are his supreme opportunity: (1) to give the lie to Satan; (2) to vindicate God under trial; (3) to demonstrate his own bare-handed loyalty— "Though He slay me, yet will I trust Him" (Job 13:15).

The mystery is further resolved when we see how Job emerges from his trials.

2—A Better Man for His Sufferings. Through it all a calm confidence sustained him, even as he assured his blind comforters: "He knoweth the way that I take: when He hath tried me, I shall come forth as gold" (Job 23:10). Job had not yet come into his best. He needed humbling for a true estimate of himself. And now, stripped of all self-righteousness and self-reliance, in true humility he cries: "I have heard of Thee by the hearing of the ear; but now mine eye seeth Thee. Wherefore I abhor myself, and repent in dust and ashes" (Job 42:5, 6).

In these words, however, is the desired master key to the mystery, namely—

3—A New Supreme Revealing of God. "Now mine eye seeth Thee." What was in that sight? (Not the glorious holiness of God as Isaiah saw Him— Isaiah 6). Something of God Job would never have known but for his sufferings. Something suited to his need. Surely it was that God is a

God of Suffering.*

He saw God as the supreme Sufferer, suffering before Job and far more than Job. It is not too much to think that in that granted sight of Himself God revealed the preexistent Cross and Himself prepared for it. He revealed "the Lamb slain from the foundation of the world" (Rev. 13:8) and Himself— a Sufferer before man ever came into existence or had opportunity to sin and suffer.

No wonder Job abhorred himself—as should all of us if tempted to complain of our small degree of suffering or to think ourselves undeserving of it.

The sequel is one of which we must not lose sight. When the divine purpose was accomplished, with a twofold restoration "the Lord blessed the latter end of Job more than the beginning" (Job 42:12). Much light is thrown upon the mystery of suffering by its priceless "afterward" (Heb. 11:11).

The Mystery of Suffering finds its truest explanation in the fact that God knew no way to make Himself fully known but through Suffering; that He deliberately and of purpose chose the way of suffering for Himself; that He invited man to share in it as our only way of truly knowing Him; that the natural yearning of His children should be to "know Him . . . and the fellowship of His sufferings" (Phil. 3:10). For the only God there is to know is the God of Suffering.

*The only person of the Godhead human eyes have ever seen is the Second Person—John 1:18; 14:9. He has always suffered, not only *for* His people but *with* His people. He revealed Himself in the fiery furnace, sharing it with the three Hebrews (Dan. 3). Saul saw Him suffering with His persecuted followers (Acts 9). By this disclosure of the Lord as his Redeemer-Sufferer Job was shamed into uncomplaining repentance.

II

SUFFERING — Its Ministry

"It is good for me that I have been afflicted"
—Ps. 119:71.

The cure for complaining is a firm conviction that the things we suffer are meant for our good, that the finer qualities of living are ministered to us in this way, that our Heavenly Father in infinite love and tenderness has appointed them for us and is Himself causing them to "work together for good." Such a persuasion saves us from the false, fatalistic philosophy that regards suffering as an inescapable evil—bear up under it the best you can.

The psalmist knew he was a better man for his affliction. His testimony should command attention. He recalls that before the experience of suffering he was going astray (Ps. 119:67). It was God's way of bringing him back—back to God, to His Word, to an upright, dutiful and devoted life.

Literally thousands upon thousands through the centuries could testify to a like experience. It will pay the reader to do some recollecting on his own account, doubtless resulting in a like testimony becoming his.

Many and varied are the benefits accruing to us through the Ministry of Suffering. We should take great care not to miss them. Of our Lord it is revealed that "though He was a Son, yet learned He obedience by the things which He suffered" (Heb. 5:8). Could sinful man think to learn in any easier way? If obedience to God is desirable, then equally to be desired is the suffering that guides our feet into it.

The Lessons of Faith

The Christian life is a life of faith, faith that functions in the dark where there is no light for sight. But such faith does not come by wishing. It is not a hothouse plant, and those who live at ease seem never to acquire it. It springs from the soil of suffering.

When God tests you He is honoring you with the opportunity of testing Him, of putting Him and His promises to the proof. "The only way to learn strong faith is to endure great trial. I have learned my faith by standing firm amid severe testing." This is the testimony of George Mueller, the 19th century Apostle of Faith.

Patience and Calm Reliance

Man is naturally impatient, easily fretted by the circumstances that vex and disappoint. Then, if he is listening, comes a voice: "Be still, and know that I am God" (Ps. 46:10). The margin reads, "Let be." Do not be fussed and perturbed; find the good of yielding in quietness of spirit to the circumstance. "Count it all joy, my brethren, when ye fall into manifold trials";—temptations, testings—"knowing that the proving of your faith worketh patience" (Jas. 1:2, 3, R. V.). Triumphantly Paul declares: "We glory in tribulations also: knowing that tribulation worketh patience; and patience, experience; and experience, hope" (Rom. 5:3, 4).

It is to the troubled heart that God speaks: "In returning and rest shall ye be saved; in quietness and in confidence shall be your strength"; but too often He must note our failure by adding, "and ye would not" (Isa. 30:15). Rather may a childlike faith whisper, "I will trust, and not be afraid" (Isa. 12:2).

The Life of Love

Selfishness is the love of self. Only the "unselfed" life really loves. That needful "unselfing" comes through Suffering. It may require physical suffering: "He that hath suffered in the flesh hath ceased from sin" (I Pet. 4:1), perhaps chiefly the sin of self-seeking. It may be the ministry of keen disappointment. The beneficent effect of such suffering is to turn one's love away from self, channelling it out in genuine, "unselfed" concern for others.

THE GIFT OF LOVE

"It is in loving, not in being loved,
    The heart is blessed;
It is in giving, not seeking gifts,
    We find our quest.

> If thou art hungry, lacking heavenly bread,
>   Give hope and cheer.
> If thou art sad and would be comforted,
>   Stay sorrow's fear.
> Whatever be thy longing, or thy need,
>   That do thou give."

Utter Dependence upon God

Sin shows itself in self-sufficiency and self-reliance. Nothing short of suffering serves to cut these props from underneath us, ministering to the heart exercised thereby a sense of need, of dependence upon God.

"Call upon Me in the day of trouble: I will deliver thee, and thou shalt glorify Me" (Ps. 50:15). Little trouble, little prayer—this is the experience of multitudes. Why pray when one is doing so well by himself? Our Heavenly Father loves us too well to let us go on living prayerless lives. Burdening trials come; they are His way of turning us to seek His face. Read, please, Psalm 107, noting its recurring refrain: "Then they cried unto the Lord in their trouble, and He saved them out of their distresses" (Ps. 107:6, 13, 19, 28).

"It is good for me that I have been afflicted; that I might learn Thy statutes" (Ps. 119:71). The ministry of Suffering is that we may listen to God, that we may learn to love His Word, delighting ourselves in it. Read the Psalms, for the most part written under the stress of trials and testings for the comfort and strengthening of those in trouble. How many saints of God have turned for unfailing solace to the twenty-third psalm: "The Lord is my shepherd; I shall not want." Drinking deeply at the fountain of living water for troubled hearts, you will thank God unceasingly for the suffering that has ministered a life of unbroken fellowship with Him.

III

SUFFERING — Sin, Satan and Self(ish)ness

*"Because thou hast done this . . . in sorrow . . .
in sorrow"*—Gen. 3:14, 16, 17.

Man has an inquiring mind. He insists on tracing things to their source. He wants to know the reason. So he asks: Whence came Suffering? and why?

In this the Bible meets him fully, devoting its first three chapters to the question of origins. They explain why things are as they are rather than as they should be. They give us what we cannot otherwise know: the origin of man, of the world in which he was placed, of all things about him, of sin, of sorrow, of suffering, of ensuing separation from God.

God made man, the Genesis record tells us, after a perfect pattern. He reproduced Himself. He made man in His own image, so that when He looked upon man He would see the likeness of Himself. He planned a person answering to Himself, one with whom He could have fellowship and constant enjoyment.

17

Then He made another human, answering to man—woman (the Hebrew is *ish* and *isha,* man and, shall we say, man more beautiful). He wanted man to have fellowship with Himself, with every possible satisfaction, nothing lacking. And to make their bliss complete He placed them in a garden, with every provision heart could wish, shut in with each other and Himself, in love unrestrained, in joy unalloyed, in happy harmony with all that life held for them.

In this, man's first estate, there was nothing to mar, nothing to vex or annoy, nothing to disappoint. There was no quarrel, no misunderstanding. There were no shadows, no suggestion of sorrow. No tears ever fell. There was no thought of suffering; no occasion for suffering; no room for suffering. Felicity complete.

Satan Drives a Wedge

But God had an enemy, hateful, subtle, vengeful. Himself fallen from fellowship with God, Satan cannot leave God free to enjoy His new and finest creation. He will inject himself into that happy garden and wreck its fellowship. Has God made man in His likeness? He will mar that likeness. Has God made man loving? He will make him hateful. Humble? he will make him proud. Knowing only good? he will make him to taste evil. Obedient? he will teach him disobedience. He will cut man loose from God; he will have man for himself.

Plotting thus, Satan entered the Garden. Boldly the serpent inveigled the woman, suggesting that she act independently of God, in fancied self-interest. She did: the man did. It was sin—sin that severed the life-cord between God and man, sin that set man on Satan's side, in a purposed state of "enmity against God." Man had fallen from a God-centered life of God-consciousness to a self-centered life of self-consciousness. Henceforth he would please, not God but himself. Man was swindled; Satan rejoiced; God sorrowed.

"But God" (Eph. 2:4); He "so loved" (John 3:16)—at whatever cost He will spend the ages repairing the damage. Satan is condemned to suffer (Gen. 3:14, 15); and He, in the "seed of the woman," will suffer even more. Woman must suffer her long, weary way (Gen. 3:16). Man must suffer the struggle of daily existence till death ends it all (Gen. 3:17-19). And since the Garden has been ruined, robbed of its fellowship, the sad picture climaxes in the words, "So He drove out the man" (Gen. 3:24)—out from the presence of God, out to a life of toil and suffering he has brought upon himself—a life in which God shares as the Chief Sufferer, till Satan is banished forever from his freedom to deceive (Rev. 20), and that lost fellowship is completely restored in the garden of eternity, where all tears are wiped away (Rev. 21, 22).

IV

SUFFERING and the Supreme Sufferer

*"His visage was so marred more than any man . . .
A man of sorrows, and acquainted with grief"*—
Isa. 52:14; 53:3.

Having traced Suffering to its source, we should be forever freed from the temptation to blame God for our sufferings. Especially is this so as we go on to see that the brunt of it all was to fall upon God as the chief Sufferer.

The catastrophe in the Garden was no surprise to God. He permitted it. Yes, He anticipated it. He had long before prepared for it. He did not risk Satan's spoiling His creation without having, ready-made, a plan adequate to meet it—a plan for completely remedying it at whatever cost of suffering to Himself.

God had His "Lamb slain from the foundation of the world" (Rev. 13:8). It was He Himself in Lamb form—all the innocence and meekness of God pitted against the pride and arrogance of Satan, triumphing over him in utter willingness to suffer.

With such a triumph in view, fully counting the cost, He purposed for Himself a flesh and blood existence, a sharing of man's lot that He might redeem man unto Himself "with the precious blood of Christ, as of a lamb without blemish and without spot: who verily was foreordained before the foundation of the world, but was manifest in these last times for you" (I Pet. 1:19, 20).

What was our lot from the Garden down? Living under a death penalty and in a state of death. "For in the day that thou eatest thereof thou shalt surely die" (Gen. 2:17). "Wherefore as by one man sin entered into the world, and death by sin; and so death passed upon all men, for that all have sinned" (Rom. 5:12). As the first Adam failed, exchanging life in God-likeness for death, God became the Second Adam to undo the power of death.

Christ came to suffer our death. Not an ordinary physical death, but also the curse and shame of it, for "Cursed is every one that hangeth on the tree" (Gal. 3:13). He suffered a death of extreme ignominy and contempt so that no murderer or harlot could ever say that God had not tasted his or her death. It was death of utmost suffering, beyond man's power to describe or understand. It was infnite God in infinite suffering.

"He is despised and rejected of men; a man of sorrows, and acquainted with grief: and we hid as it were our faces from Him; He was despised, and we esteemed Him not. Surely He hath borne our griefs,and carried our sorrows: yet we did esteem Him stricken, smitten of God, and afflicted.

But He was wounded for our transgressions, He was bruised for our iniquities: the chastisement of our peace was upon Him; and with His stripes we are healed. All we like sheep have gone astray; we have turned every one to his own way; and the Lord hath laid on Him the iniquity of us all" (Isa. 53:3-6).

But the marvel of it grows upon us when we consider how few among men really care. "Is it nothing to you, all ye that pass by?" that such a Sufferer suffers for you? Who cares? A mere handful of believers out of the billions of earth for whom He died, agonizing in their stead. What added suffering, that they spurn His love! Yet He knew they would. Such love, prompting such suffering, in the face of mass rejection, is beyond all comprehension.

But we are considering the problem of Suffering, and we must follow it to its conclusion. If a loving, righteous God knew no way out but to visit such untold suffering upon Himself—that is exactly what Calvary is—what will that God require at the hands of those who will not let His Sufferer suffer in their stead? Of those bringing added sorrow and shame upon Him?

Though but little realized, a rejected Calvary is the touchstone of the world's mounting woes today. To see this is to have much light shed upon the puzzling problem of present-day suffering.

Sooner or later—most likely sooner it would seem—society's woes will climax in what is termed the Great Tribulation. Nearly all the prophets give it unusual prominence. Jesus described it as beyond anything known to history, so severe that only a shortening of the time will enable men to survive (Matt. 24:15-22). How lightly men toss aside these solemn words of warning; then they complain that they cannot understand their multiplied woes and distresses, increasing as these predicted days of sorrow draw nearer.

The Three Cups

In the above we have been gaining a dispensational view of Suffering, short only of its eternal aspect. Eternal suffering is merely the projection into eternity of that state of separation from God which man has brought upon himself and which his unbelief refuses to terminate by an acceptance of the sufferings of God in his behalf.

This is made exceedingly plain through the three "cups" referred to in the New Testament. A cup represents one's lot in life. Thus we have three different lots clearly distinguished in: His Cup; Our Cup; Their Cup.

1—His Cup (Matt. 26:39; John 18:11). This cup was pressed to the lips of our Lord Jesus Christ. It contained the greatest sufferings ever known to man—sufferings physical, mental, spiritual. Though He was sinless, He was to be "made sin for us." Though He was the Lord of Life, He was to "taste death for every man." Though He lived in the constant favor of His Father, that Father's very presence was to be withdrawn from Him—"forsaken" because He was to receive the stroke due to us—God's wrath for sin. That's the Cross; that's Calvary; that is His cup.

2—Our Cup (Matt. 26:27, 28; I Cor. 11:25). In His cup Jesus drank the very dregs of our sin and the full wrath of God due to us for it. He emptied it of wrath that He might offer us a cup filled with love and grace. It is the "cup of the new covenant" or agreement between God and man. It is called the communion cup; that is, the cup of restored fellowship, of constant, unbroken fellowship between God and those who partake of it. This, our cup, is the pledge that we will never suffer God's wrath for sin—Christ did that for us—nor ever be separated from His loving favor.

All that we who enjoy this cup of divine love may ever suffer should be viewed and weighed in the light of this glorious fact.

3—Their Cup (Rev. 14:10; 16:19; 17:4; 18:6). This is a cup of wrath, called "the cup of His indignation." Indignation that men should treat His Son and His Sufferings with scorn. Indignation that men should side with His enemy in bringing added ruin to this woe-beset earth. Men on all sides have despised the Blood of Calvary as the way back to God. He bought the Church with His own blood (Acts 20:28); that blood is most precious in His sight. Yet the spurning of that blood is the hardened and settled attitude of men everywhere. Soon must God say, "Men will not have My sufferings for their sin. They will not come back to Me. It is time for them to drink their own cup of woe, to taste their own sorrows."

The holocausts of world wars have caused much questioning: Why such suffering? Why doesn't God intervene? God did intervene centuries ago. Calvary accepted, such wars and such sufferings could not be. The human family has not yet matched the sufferings of God. However great man's woes to date, through them He is warning that greater sorrows are impending ere the complete solution of man's sin and waywardness is reached.

V

SUFFERING as a Father's Chastening

"Whom the Lord loveth He chasteneth . . . If ye endure chastening God dealeth with you as with sons"—
Heb. 12:6, 7.

Suffering takes on a very different meaning when we see in it our Father's hand, His loving tenderness toward us, purposing only "our profit" (vs. 10).

If we would fortify ourselves with the greatest possible encouragement under trial, we should read and ponder Hebrews 12:5-11. Herein is revealed to our hearts that the very fact of our suffering is a matter for genuine gratification. It is the evidence that God recognizes our sonship to Him and is dealing with us as sons. He counts us as members of His family and, like any father, He wants us to amount to something. He is bringing out the possibilities He sees in us. What more can we desire?

By the same token, if we lack chastening we have abundant reason for discouragement. We may not be His sons, only "bastards" whom He does not care to own. Or, possibly, He's not planning to make anything much of us—just the ordinary run, unsuited to any real usefulness. (Something to think about, isn't it?)

Chastening Is Child-Training Discipline

The Greek for chastening is a compounded word meaning "child-training." From our yielding to the discipline of earthly fathers we are led up to the "much rather" of subjection to our Heavenly Father. If they saw faults in us, calling for "correction," how much more He. If their love desired our best, even though at the price of suffering to us—woodshed sessions, possibly—how much more He.

Few of us realize how far short we come of our Father's standards, and how much our shortcomings remind Him of Eden's marring. Glad for being brought back into His family, we should be grateful indeed for the strokes that mould and shape us into worthiness to be His sons, imparting qualities that reflect the family traits of character.

Self-Will or His Will

The essence of father-son relationship is obedience. The one barrier to obedience is the setting up of the child's will against the parent's. The securing of obedience is merely a matter of conforming the will of the child to the will of the parent.

It was here, let us recall, that man separated himself from God—he acted in self-will, in self-interest, setting aside God's expressed will for his own will. There and then human life descended to a self-willed level. It is in the thinking of all of us—in the blood. Only by much discipline do we attain the "unselfed" life, the life of full conformity, of unbroken fellowship.

Of our Lord, to our amazement it is recorded: "Though He were a Son, yet learned He obedience by the things which He suffered" (Heb. 5:8). The most perfect life, flesh and blood based, required the discipline of suffering to escape self-will and keep in sinless conformity to His Father's will. Every step spelled self-renunciation. At length in Gethsemane came the test of supreme suffering, attested by the blood-sweat of His agony. Would He act in self-interest, for self-deliverance? In that hour came the cry that delighted the Father's heart: "Not My will, but Thine." The Son had triumphed; so had the Father—in Him. There was life on earth utterly "unselfed."

Dear suffering one, read a Father's love into your sorrows and disappointments. Never resist. Never resent. Just yield. Believe and know that He is working all for your good—He loves you so. Glimpse the higher goal He has in view for you, even through the tears of cherished plans dashed into the dust.

Remember, He wants the fellowship of Eden restored. He wants your child-life Father-centered. It hasn't been. Many a prized possession has come between. Many a plan, many an ambition has been yours, not His for you. He loves you, and whom He

loves He chastens into an "unselfed" way of living.
His love is bent on having you for Himself, that He
may delight Himself in you.

Before your Father's perfect love and perfect
will for you, lay down your self-life without another
struggle. Count it settled. Let it not seem hard.
Having done so, in the fellowship that follows life
will become sweet and satisfying, with a sense of
carefreeness. You are His Child. You and your
Father are in full accord. To your yielded heart He
ministers new joy, new peace, new patience. Rejoice! You are on the way to be "to the praise of the
glory of His grace."

VI

SUFFERING as a Purifier

"He shall sit as a refiner and purifier of silver"—
Mal. 3:3.

The process of conformity involves more by far than mere willingness; it's a question of fitness. The work must go deeper. It must go back of the will to the desires that move upon and motivate the will.

Sin made us a something "by nature" that we should not have been. Sin corrupted our nature; it must be cleansed. Sin polluted our nature; it must be purged. Sin warped and twisted our nature; it must be straightened. Sin marred the divine image; it must be restored. Can this be done without suffering?

It is common observation that the mere acceptance of Christ as Saviour, in itself involving a miracle in the soul that works a marvelous change, too often leaves this needful transformation far from complete. With many the process seems to become halted, stopped short, stalemated. Its purpose is thwarted. Life flows on in the normal channel of

30

creature comforts and material conveniences, of possessions that make these possible, of the enjoyments that accompany them. The aim of Christian living, the ultimate of Christian character—these are lost and forgotten.

Chosen in the Furnace of Affliction

But God steps in, and the picture is changed. Suffering stalks the pathway. And God speaks: "I have chosen you in the furnace of affliction" (Isa. 48:10). In the light of Eden's comforts, issuing in such miserable failure; in the light of Calvary's sufferings, issuing in such glorious triumph, is He harsh? or kind?

What is the furnace for? For suffering? Oh, no! For the separation brought about by suffering. In Eden's fall man became a mixture of "good and evil" (Gen. 3:22). But God recovered us to Himself to be a peculiar treasure, that is, a treasure peculiar to Himself and precious. To enjoy the preciousness He must refine away what He sees as worthless dross. "I will turn My hand upon thee, and purely purge away thy dross, and take away all thy tin" (Isa. 1:25).

"And He shall sit as a refiner and purifier of silver: and He shall purify . . . and purge them as gold and silver" (Mal. 3:3). How intense shall the heat be? and how long shall it last? The refiner sits at his task, bending over, watching intently till he sees his likeness mirrored back to him. So with our Refiner. The furnace is not for suffering; it is for Christ-likeness through suffering. Would you have the likeness? Gladly go through the furnace under His loving eye.

> "Is there no other way, O God,
>   Except through sorrow, pain and loss,
> To stamp Christ's likeness on my soul—
> No other way except the cross?
>
> And then a voice stills all my soul,
>   As stilled the waves of Galilee:
> 'Canst thou not bear the furnace heat,
>   If 'mid the flames I walk with thee?
>
> 'I bore the cross, I know its weight,
>   I drank the cup I hold for thee;
> Canst thou not follow where I lead?
>   I'll give thee strength—lean hard on Me.'"

Separated by suffering! Human nature being such as it is, there is seemingly no other way. This is further illustrated by the threshing-floor. While growing in the field the chaff is joined to the wheat. The two must be threshed into separation. In Bible times oxen walked over the grain-covered floor or a flail was used to smite it, to bruise it, to crush it apart. The process spelled suffering. Then came the sifting; the "fan" lifted it to the wind which carried the light chaff away.

Dear one, are you being bruised? and sifted too? Do not shrink from it. See the Hand of love holding the fan. Be assured He has a worthwhile purpose in it all. He counts you precious. He wants to have you to cherish and treasure, apart from what He counts but chaff. Let Him have His perfect way.

The Vessel Re-Made

It has pleased our God, in recovering humanity from the wreckage of Eden to a life of fellowship with Him and usefulness to Him, to put "this treasure" of His presence "in earthen vessels, that the exceeding greatness of the power might be" of Himself and not from us (II Cor. 4:7). That we may know something of the re-making required, we are taken to the potter's house. We see him occupied with a vessel that has been marred. Does he throw it into the discard? No, indeed. He puts it on his wheel and re-shapes it, his skill imparting to it the perfection and beauty he has in his mind for it. And as we stand there, watching the process to which the clay is subjected, the Lord our Potter whispers to us: "Can I not do with you as this potter?" (Jer. 18:1-6).

But more. To this suffering with beauty and correction in view, there must be added a suffering for permanence and endurance. Now comes the firing, and the re-firing—the more times the more value imparted. The Master's design must be burnt in; then no evil-bent world touch can leave its marring imprint.

Does the process seem long to you? Too severe? Too uncomfortable? Wholly trust your Refiner—He is intent upon the pure gold. (Read and mark in your Bible Job 23:10). Wholly trust the One presiding at His threshing-floor—He seeks the separated wheat. Wholly trust your skilled Potter—He wants a vessel of beauty such as He can delight to use.

Saturate your mind and heart with His Word. In its pages much is made plain. Not only will it comfort and sustain you; it will serve to hasten and facilitate the purifying work. Through it you will catch a vision of His high purposes for you—all that He is aiming at—nothing short of His own likeness, wrought out of the rough.

You may have visited Rushmore Mountain in western South Dakota and stood gazing across the chasm at the noble faces of our great men carved from the natural rock. You may have seen the sculptor busy at his work, bringing out the features of a man. You may have thought of him as saying: "Each blow of the hammer, each sharp cutting of the chisel, each rough chip that falls—all bring the likeness nearer to realization."

Dear reader, instead of shrinking from the suffering involved, share, will you not, the Master Workman's eager enthusiasm for the ideal He has in mind for you. Work with Him. Lend yourself fully, unflinchingly, to whatever it takes.

A bar of iron, worth only $1 in the rough, by submitting to the suffering required for real usefulness, takes on unbelievable value. Worked into horseshoes, it is worth $2; into needles, $70; into pen-knife blades, $650; into watch springs, $50,000! Its worth is proportionate to the grilling. How it must be hammered, and fired, and pounded, heated again to a white heat, re-shaped and polished, to become at length 50,000 times as valuable as in its natural pre-suffering state.

VII

SUFFERING the Path to Sympathizing

"Be ye all likeminded, sympathetic (Gk), loving as brethren, tenderhearted, humbleminded"—
I Pet. 3:8, R.V.

From Eden on down human life is basically self-interested and self-centered. We would fain coin a word to describe it—a state of "selfness." Man being such as he is, suffering becomes an absolute necessity for the breaking down of the barrier of self-interest and the creating of a genuine heart concern for others.

It is much to be doubted whether life on this globe would be endurable but for the tendering of the hardness of the human heart through sorrow, trial and disappointment; through sickness and infirmity that halt and limit the proud, self-reliant spirit; through the oft thwarting of selfish ambitions, perchance through the loss of possessions and with them their power for self-gratification.

If, in spite of all the suffering and its tendering influences, men still fight and squabble as they do, what would this world be if there were no suffering and none of its softening restraints? It utterly baffles the imagination.

The answer to this native, inherent "selfness" is the Christian life in its full realization. "I have been crucified with Christ; and it is no longer I that live, but Christ liveth in me" (Gal. 2:20, R.V.*) "We thus judge, that one died for all, therefore all died; and He died for all, that they that live should no longer live unto themselves, but unto Him who for their sakes died and rose again" (II Cor. 5:14, 15, R.V.). "To me to live is Christ" (Phil. 1:21). Thus the Christian life contemplates and provides for an absolute change of center—not I, but Christ. The Christian life is the "unselfed" life.

But—is it? Observation answers, No. The average Christian—possibly yourself included—has never made the change. Self is tenacious of his rights; he claims a life-tenure. He holds to the saddle and rides on to gain his ambitious goal.

It is here that Suffering enters—enters for the deposing of Mr. Self. Then in turn God enters— enters as He was never privileged to do before, for the comforting and strengthening that meets and matches the suffering. "Who comforteth us in all our tribulation, that we may be able to comfort them who are in any trouble, by the comfort where-with we ourselves are comforted of God" (II Cor. 1:4).

God's comfort, then, is not intended just to make us comfortable. It terminates not upon us, but upon others. "Whether we be afflicted, it is for your consolation" (II Cor. 1:6). Our God has thus attained His twofold purpose. The life is "unselfed" through suffering, and the sufferer has become a sympathizer.

Sympathize means to "suffer with." We do not suffer alone, nor do we leave our fellows to suffer alone—we suffer together. Our hearts flow together; they harmonize; brotherly love draws them into a common bond of understanding. They are united in a fellowship of suffering.

Then, if we have not suffered in vain; if we know the comfort; if we have experienced the heart cure, we have reached a degree of usefulness in this sorrowing world to be found in no other way.

Just as in radio the sending and receiving instruments must be harmonized, tuned each to the other, so in human life. Suffering does the tuning, fitting the heart life of one into that of his fellow. Happy indeed the one who has so profited by his sorrows, pains, trials and disappointments as to have become a sending instrument in the Lord's hands. Multitudes in this stricken world are on the receiving end.

We have seen it time and again. The one who has suffered and known its "profit"—to such the steps of the needy, the sorrowing, the discouraged are drawn as by a magnet. They go to avail themselves of attentive ears and understanding heart, made so by suffering akin to theirs, assured that back to them will come the needed help. If you have entered the school of suffering, make sure of your U.S. degree—Understanding Sympathizer.

VIII

SUFFERING as a Christian

"But if any man suffer as a Christian, let him not be ashamed; but let him glorify God in this name"—
I Pet. 4:16, R.V.

Up to this point we have been occupied with the problem of Suffering: *Why* should we suffer? We have seen that, having a God such as He is, in a world such as it is, human nature being as it is, there is much reason for suffering and much profit from suffering.

Now we turn to the further, practical question: *How* should we suffer? It is here that Peter has much help for us. Peter is the New Testament expositor of Suffering. He sees the Christian in an unfriendly world—just passing through. He would have us geared to suffering, expecting it and prepared for it. Others suffer, justly and unjustly. The Christian lives in the same world—a world of suffering. Has he purchased immunity from it?

What does it mean to "suffer as a Christian"? (1) To accept willingly whatever suffering of whatever nature may be our lot because we are Christian, as others suffer for being a murderer, a thief or an evildoer (I Pet. 4:15). (2) To display the attitude toward our suffering and the spirit in our suffering that become a Christian. We should—

1—**Suffer Uncomplainingly.** In this the Israelites passing through the wilderness set a negative example for us—read I Cor. 10:1-13. They murmured; they complained; they found fault with their lot, with their leaders and with their Redeemer God, bringing upon themselves the divine displeasure. Learning from them, let us cheerfully trust through it all, expecting to experience His grace sustaining us and His hand delivering us (vs. 13).

2—**Suffer Unresistingly.** The set, unbending, unyielding attitude, unwilling to accept the trial without a struggle, not crediting a Heavenly Father with loving wisdom—such an attitude is a refusal to "suffer according to the will of God" (I Pet. 4:19). It is not only un-Christian; it is great spiritual loss. The trial was sent to train us in the yielded life. Only a constant yielding can produce a yielded life. Resisting is refusing to learn. In this, nature becomes our teacher. The unbending pole snaps before the storm. The oak, yielding to its smitings, acquires sturdiness and strength of fiber. Today the oak's ability to withstand the storm is an object lesson in how to suffer.

3—**Suffer Undeservedly.** In this we grievously fail our great Leader in Suffering. Read very thoughtfully I Pet. 2:19-24. If we suffer patiently for our wrongdoing there is nothing praiseworthy in that—it's what we deserve. But if, when we do well and suffer for it, we endure patiently, this is acceptable with God (vs. 20). Why? Now we are suffering undeservedly. This is Christian. This is Christlike. This is fitting into the pattern—the example of suffering He left for us. To this kind of suffering, to this manner of suffering we are called (vs. 21).

Having read these searching words from Peter's pen, reading on we have brought to mind our Saviour's attitude under suffering utterly undeserved (vv. 22-24). We behold Him in Pilate's judgment hall, faced with the greatest injustice ever heaped upon a man. We see our Saviour as our example: in His sufferings for us, uncomplaining, unresisting, undeserving. And that calm, majestic figure calls to us: "Follow Me."

4—Suffer with Christ and for Christ. It is glorious to know that our Christ not only suffered *for* us but even today is suffering *with* us. To those who would hurt His own He cries, "Why persecutest thou Me?" We are given to see Him walking amidst the candlesticks, sharing the lot of His suffering saints (Rev. 1:13). "In all their affliction He was afflicted" (Isa. 63:9). He suffering with us, and we not with Him? and for Him? "Inasmuch as ye did it not to one of these, ye did it not to Me" (Matt. 25:45).

With this background for Christian living how natural and rightful that we should "go forth therefore unto Him . . . bearing His reproach" (Heb. 13:13). Paul regards the multiplicity of his sufferings—II Cor. 4:8-18; 6:1-10—as a sharing with his Lord and Saviour, supplying what might be lacking in the personal sufferings of Christ (Gal. 6:17; Col. 1:24). If Christ the Head suffered in His day upon earth, how should His body suffer in our day! So Paul writes from prison: "To you it hath been granted in the behalf of Christ, not only to believe on Him, but also to suffer in His behalf" (Phil. 1:29, R.V.) What we are accustomed to call service—doing this or that—by no means comprehends the calling of a Christian. Sharing in suffering we most truly serve.

5—Suffer Rejoicingly. Here is a height left unscaled by most of us moderns. The early Christians, arrested and berated, were found "rejoicing that they were counted worthy to suffer dishonor for the Name" (Acts 5:41, R.V.). Of Christian people Paul says that "We also rejoice in our tribulations" (Rom. 5:3, R.V.). And the midnight praises from the Philippian prison, while their backs were smarting and bleeding, attested that Paul and Silas practiced rejoicing in suffering. If Paul taught us that we should "rejoice always" (I Thess. 5:16, R.V.) it was only because he himself lived it, as he testifies of his own experience of suffering: "As sorrowful, yet always rejoicing" (II Cor. 6:10, Peter likewise insists that Christians regard their "fiery trial" not as a "strange thing" but as an occasion for rejoicing, here and hereafter: "But rejoice, inasmuch as ye are partakers of Christ's sufferings; that, when His glory shall be revealed, ye may be glad also with exceeding joy" (I Pet. 4:13).

> *"Sometimes a light surprises*
> *The Christian while he sings."*

IX

SUFFERING and God's "Afterwards"

"Now no chastening for the present seemeth to be joyous, but grievous; nevertheless afterward it yieldeth the peaceable fruit of righteousness unto them which are exercised thereby"—Heb.. 12:11.
"Our light affliction . . . worketh for us"
—II Cor. 4:17.

Opportunity! Men complain of lack of opportunity. Opportunity for what? If we desire to be unusual, developed out of the ordinary, Suffering is the open door of opportunity. To be something we never could hope to be; to *know* what otherwise we would not know; to *do* what others are incapable of doing—this is Suffering's "afterward."

Trial and trouble, sorrow and loss, suffering and heartache, pain and disappointment "work for us" among the "all things" of Romans 8:28. With a negative half-belief we have imagined it might be; but we wouldn't eagerly welcome or invite such experiences. Why be so foolish? Rather, we would

42

do everything to avoid them, quite willing to miss their "afterward."

We think of a Saul of Tarsus—learned university graduate, prominent "churchman," "suffering the loss of all things," becoming known to posterity, like his Lord, as a "man of sorrows"—leaving us a clear-cut testimony as to God's "afterward":

> "*Most gladly therefore will I rather glory in my infirmities, that the power of Christ may rest upon me. Therefore, I take pleasure in infirmities, in reproaches, in necessities, in persecutions, in distresses for Christ's sake; for when I am weak, then am I strong*" (II Cor. 12:9, 10).

We think of a George Matheson, doomed to loss of sight, only to suffer the added anguish of human love's desertion—the refusal to marry a blind man. God's "afterward" has come down to us in his—

> *O Love that wilt not let me go,*
> *I rest my weary soul in Thee;*
> *I give Thee back the life I owe,*
> *That in Thine ocean depths its flow*
> *May richer, fuller be.*

We think of an Annie Johnson Flint, suffering such pain of body, only that she might know His peace and joy of heart, telling it out to countless thousands:

> I KNOW—*this one triumphant word*
> *Can silence doubts and banish fears;*
> *I know that all things work for good*
> *And I have proved it through the years.**

*From the poem *I Know* in *Songs of Faith and Comfort*. Used by permission of Evangelical Publishers, Toronto, Canada.

We think of Fannie Crosby, her eyes blinded that in the dark she might see and know and tell the riches of the unseen world:

> *Perfect submission, all is at rest,*
> *I in my Saviour am happy and blest;*
> *Watching and waiting, looking above,*
> *Filled with His goodness, lost in His love.*

Talk with mothers and they will tell what the sufferings, sorrows and sacrifices of motherhood have meant to them, making them unselfish, kind, thoughtful and considerate of others. Thus is the curse of Eden turned to great spiritual blessing. One mother recounts how she fought having a family—too self-centered to be bothered with it; today she is one of the sweetest mothers of the land, a queen in a truly Christian home.

A girl who was an auto accident shut-in for 13 years gives her testimony:

During these years the Lord has done glorious things for me. First, He saved me. It was through being cut off from the normal affairs of a young person's life that the Lord could get me to listen to Him. How I thank Him for His patience in dealing with my rebellious heart! He has satisfied me moment by moment, making what would be a dull, monotonous life into one of joyous praise, all because of His presence in my life. I wouldn't take anything for the experience of these 13 years. I know the sufficiency of the Lord in a way I would never have known otherwise. One of my favorite verses is Ps. 37:4: "Delight thyself also in the Lord; and He shall give thee the desires of thine heart."

A young man's body was rendered as rigid as a board by the ravages of disease. He devoted himself to a study of God's Word. The Lord gave him a Bible class that gathered regularly in a circle about his bed. A sense of peace, joy and contentment pervaded his room.

Here's a family who suffered the loss by fire of all their earthly possessions. Today they testify it proved a rare blessing in teaching a quiet, confident trust in God, with constant contentment with their lot and continual praise for a Heavenly Father's provision for them.

In Michigan there lived a woman for 14 years bedridden with arthritis. It had left her knees drawn up toward her face and her hands crippled like two clubs. On the wall there hung a map of the world. Every morning by prayer she made the trip around the world. Was there a God's "afterward"? The testimony of a devoted pastor is that standing in her presence he felt sorry for himself in his lack of the joy and the praise he saw displayed in the sufferer's life.

One whose life has been a succession of trials, of struggles and disappointments, has through them become most useful. With no help but in God she learned to live in utter dependence upon His Word. She says:

I have learned through suffering that Christ is our sufficiency during any trial or testing. He becomes more precious as the fires of testing burn away the dross and melt the heart to yield all to His blessed will. Phil. 4:13 has been proven true through many years of varied testings. How I thank God for II Cor. 9:8 and I Cor. 10:13. Daniel 3 shows the three Hebrews thrown into the fiery furnace "bound," but the fire burned off their bonds, enabling them to "walk" with the Son of God. When sorrows and disappointments have overtaken me, to the Book I have gone, seeking comfort and courage. Never was there a time when the Lord failed to speak peace and give strength. With the Psalmist I can say, "Great peace have they that love Thy law (word); and nothing shall offend them" (Ps. 119:165). He comforts us, only that we might learn to comfort others (II Cor. 1:3-5). Various friends have said, "Because you are understanding I am bringing my grief to you." Thus our trials are His instrument, shaping us for service here and preparing us to reign with Him. Through abounding trials He gives superabundant grace to be overcomers, that we may attain an abundant entrance into His everlasting kingdom.

One who has served much and suffered much testifies to a resulting "confidence in God's judgment in giving just what is best," saying,

Suffering sweetens, strengthens, mellows, makes one more sympathetic, more considerate of others, more mindful of His will and eager for it. But more gratifying than all these is the sense of living in the "secret place of the Most High"—secretly passing through experiences which He alone has shared, the common knowledge of which makes me, with David, "His beloved"; and makes Him to me the One "altogether lovely," the Source of everything I ever have needed or ever can need. Suffering with Him upholding and comforting me has taught my soul to sing incessantly,

"Thou, O Christ, art all I want;
More than all in Thee I find."

There's a young man who, but a few years ago, was careless, worldly, resisting the Spirit's conviction of sin. One night on the dance floor, like Jacob of old, the Lord touched his thigh. He became a bed-ridden sufferer, undergoing extreme pain. Dependent upon the radio, one day he listened to a gospel message and was wonderfully saved. He has become a student of God's Word and a blessing to all. His testimony is that the Lord opens heaven's windows and pours out blessings to him till he can scarcely contain the joy.

We think of the blessing imparted by a parishioner who in early girlhood was afflicted with a rare disease, ossifying the flesh—anything touching her brought intense pain. Yet Annie's room was the sunshine spot of the home. One was drawn to it as by a magnet, there to enjoy the actual radiance of her joyous face and the sweet cheeriness of her voice.

One who has pased through deep waters, only to face a living sorrow, led thereby to lay aside all social and intellectual pride of life for a life instead of utter devotion to the things of Christ, out of her transforming experience brings these lines of exhortation to a friend in inconsolable sorrow:

> *I counsel thee too, sad one,*
> *Go with thy heart and gaze*
> *Again, at God's bruis-ed Son—*
> *Whose ways are not our ways.*
>
> *Look long . . . till in Love divine*
> *Thy bitter tears distill—*

Then . . . deep in those wounds hide thine,
And learn—how sweet His will.

—E. M. B.

A cousin suffered the loss of sight. One unacquainted with her secret would wonder at her unfailing overflow of joyous spirit. She had committed some 500 Scripture verses to memory; in repeating them she was constantly drinking at the fountain of divine comfort and strength.

Yielded through Suffering

For years a young woman was threatened with paralysis of the limbs. And now it has done its grievous work. Molded through intense suffering into a radiant Christian, she gives to God's people her triumphant testimony:

The most valuable lessons learned through my suffering are the priceless gems of God's marvelous mercy, love and grace. To become reconciled was no easy task and could not have been accomplished in one's own strength. The easy way would have been to give up and grumble; but that would never have produced quietness of soul with peace of mind. I recall some months before my husband passed away—he was soon to leave us, we knew, and I was growing more paralyzed every day—our earthly possessions had taken wings. Seemingly there wasn't one bit of hope and my spirit fell into complete darkness for a short while—with a bleeding heart, exhausted nerves, nothing in sight but helplessness and sorrow. I cried, "Though He slay me yet will I trust him!" Amidst all in flowed strength and comfort.

God has a glorious work to do in every yielded life, and often our heartaches and trials lead us to see the nothingness of self and the wonders of Him. Each morning after trying, sleepless nights I pray for grace to be sweet—to be still in His will. Unless one has had the experience one cannot understand the wonders of the inflowing grace. My main concern is not whether I shall be permitted to walk again, but the salvation of the priceless souls of men. "Must I go and empty handed, must I meet my Saviour so?" Often exhaustion is so great I cannot pray. At such times one word is sufficient—"ALL." He knows and understands that I am placing my "all" on the altar.

When drugs and massage fail, as they often do, in comes a song in the night, which changes my countenance from a frown to a smile. Hundreds of nights my heart has sung,

"Lord, I would have Thyself in all Thy beauty,
Take Thou control of all my life just now,
In Thee to live and move and have my being,
With full abandon, Lord, to Thee I bow."

The Man who died for me makes no mistakes. When He gives us grace to be satisfied in our affliction—and He does—then there is no affliction. Suffering has led me into a greater desire for His will, His purpose and plan for my life, than any other experience. It produces a fortitude which cannot be purchased with gold. Great are the moments, the quiet hours of waiting on Him, longing to abandon everything Christ cannot approve.

Hannah R. Higgens of Australia suffered severely from a strange and baffling disease that eventually caused the loss of one leg and both arms. Letters and cards were received from her, written most legibly by means of an apparatus (revealed to her by prayer) fitted to her shoulder. Friends found her not only patient in suffering but consistently praising and rejoicing in hope of the glory of God. Her joy in the Lord filled her room with sunshine. Those who came to comfort her left feeling that she had cheered and comforted them. "As her tribulations abounded, so her consolations did much more abound." She carried on an almost world-wide ministry of Christian cheer to missionaries, sufferers and others. Her book, "Cloud and Sunshine," closes with these words:

Looking back I marvel at my Heavenly Father's and the Lord Jesus' loving kindness to me during so many years of suffering and helplessness. I have been a sufferer nearly all my life, and now am over 77 years old, and unable to walk at all for over 46½ years . . . I still lose my voice every night; it returns during the day. I call this "Thanksgiving Corner" because I do thank and praise my loving Saviour every day for helping me to bear constant pain and weariness, and with His constant help I am happy, too. . . . Although writing is more and more difficult I shall do my bit, sending out messages to fellow sufferers and other troubled ones. . . . I long for all to prove, as I do, that with our loving Saviour's help it is possible to be happy under very trying circumstances.

X

SUFFERING — Some Practical Suggestions

Just because one suffers is no assurance that the transforming effects narrated above will follow. The result may be exactly the opposite. If one takes his suffering in the wrong way, with a resentful spirit, without divine help, it will be so. Some have become embittered for life. Some have committed suicide. Others live on in discouragement and uselessness.

The key to blessing, then, is not in suffering but in suffering the right way. It's a fine art. So few really know how. We offer these practical helps:

1—Renew Your Confidence in God.
"We know that all things work together for good to them that love God" (Rom. 8:28). "Many are the afflictions of the righteous: but the Lord delivereth him out of them all (Ps. 34:19). "Great is Thy faithfulness" (Lam. 3:23). "For I the Lord thy God will hold thy right hand, saying unto thee, Fear not, I will help thee' (Isa. 41:13). "Thou wilt keep him in perfect peace, whose mind is stayed on Thee: because he trusteth in Thee" (Isa. 26:3).

51

"Cast thy burden upon the Lord, and He shall sustain thee" (Ps. 55:22). "Though He slay me, yet will I trust in Him" (Job 13:15). Read also Isa. 41:10; 43:1, 2.

2—Pray—Earnestly, Definitely, Believingly.

"Is any among you afflicted? let him pray" (Jas. 5:13). "Men ought always to pray, and not to faint" (Lk. 18:1). "Call upon Me in the day of trouble: I will deliver thee, and thou shalt glorify Me" (Ps. 50:15). "This poor man cried, and the Lord heard him, and saved him out of all his troubles" (Ps. 34:6).

3—Count on the Spiritual Values Accruing to You.

"Reckon it nothing but joy, my brethren, whenever you find yourselves hedged by various temptations. Be assured that the testing of your faith leads to power of endurance" (Jas. 1:2, 3, Weymouth*). "We glory in tribulations also: knowing that tribulation worketh patience; and patience, experience; and experience, hope" (Rom. 5:3, 4). "Before I was afflicted I went astray: but now have I kept Thy Word. . . . It is good for me that I have been afflicted; that I might learn Thy statutes. . . . I know, O Lord, that Thy judgments are right, and that Thou in faithfulness hast afflicted me" (Ps. 119:67, 71, 75). "Behold, happy is the man whom God correcteth: therefore despise not thou the chastening of the Almighty. . . . He knoweth the way that I take: when He hath tried me, I shall come forth as gold" (Job 5:17; 23: 10).

*From *The New Testament in Modern Speech* by Richard Francis Weymouth. The Pilgrim Press. Used by permission.

4—Saturate Your Mind and Heart with God's Word.

"Comfort ye, comfort ye My people" (Isa 40:1). ". . . that we through patience and comfort of the scriptures might have hope" (Rom. 15:4). "This is my comfort in my affliction: for Thy word hath quickened me" (Ps. 119:50). "Thy word is a lamp unto my feet and a light unto my path" (Ps. 119:105). "The Lord is my shepherd; I shall not want" (Ps. 23:1). "Content with such things as ye have: for Himself hath said, I will in no wise fail thee, neither will I in any wise forsake thee. So that with good courage we say, The Lord is my helper; I will not fear: What shall man do unto me?" (Heb. 13:5, 6, R.V.). "Blessed are all they that take refuge in Him" (Ps. 2:12, R.V.). Read the Psalms repeatedly.

5—Practice Praising the Lord in the Dark.

"Who giveth songs in the night" (Job 35:10). "In the night watches" (Ps. 63:5, 6). "At midnight (backs bleeding, feet fast in the stocks) Paul and Silas prayed, and sang praises unto God: and the prisoners heard them" (Acts 16:25, with Ps. 34:1, 2). "My mouth shall praise Thee with joyful lips: when I remember Thee upon my bed, and meditate on Thee in the night watches" (Ps. 63:5, 6). "Rejoice always; pray without ceasing; in everything give thanks: for this is the will of God in Christ Jesus to you-ward" (I Thess. 5:16-18, R.V.). "Neither be ye sorry; for the joy of the Lord is your strength" (Neh. 8:10).

6—Forget Yourself in Love and Care for Others.

"Bear ye one another's burdens, and so fulfill the

law of Christ" (Gal. 6:2). "Relieve the necessities of the saints" (Rom. 12:13, Weymouth). "Rejoice with them that do rejoice, and weep with them that weep" (Rom. 12:15). "He that winneth souls is wise" (Prov. 11:30). "It is more blessed to give than to receive" (Acts 20:35).

7—Dedicate Yourself to God for a Life of Victory.
"Yield yourselves unto God." "Present your bodies a living sacrifice, holy, acceptable unto God, which is your reasonable service" (Rom. 6:13; 12:1). "Who shall separate us from the love of Christ? Shall tribulation, or distress, or persecution, or famine, or nakedness, or peril or sword? Nay, in all these things we are more than conquerors through Him that loved us" (Rom. 8:35, 37). "God is able to make all grace abound toward you; that ye, always having all sufficiency in all things, may abound to every good work" (II Cor. 9:8).

Keep Looking Up

XI

SUFFERING and Glory

"Our light affliction, which is but for a moment, worketh for us a far more exceeding and eternal weight of glory"—II Cor. 4:17. *"If so be that we suffer with Him, that we may be also glorified together"*—Rom. 8:17.

Best of all, Suffering in the will of God is our passport into promised glory as seen in the above scriptures. So did our Lord esteem His supreme suffering: "The hour is come that the Son of man should be glorified" (John 12:23). Anticipating the experience He prayed: "Father, the hour is come; glorify Thy Son" (John 17:1). Looking back upon the experience He reasoned with His doubting disciples: "Ought not Christ to have suffered these things, and to enter into His glory?" (Lk. 24:26).

Viewed, in this perspective Suffering has lost its sting. We can even welcome it—we should—chariot of fire though it be, as sweeping us into the eternal kingdom with an abundant entrance. The apostles encouraged the early Christians, as we of today should encourage one another: "that we must through much tribulation enter into the kingdom of God" (Acts 14:22).

Scripture constantly links the Suffering and the Glory. The mesage of the prophets is summarized as "the sufferings of Christ and the glory that should follow" (I Pet. 1:11). The two were brought together in His experience of transfiguration: what the disciples heard concerned "His decease"; what they saw was a foretaste of "His glory" (Lk. 9:31, 32). The Father was giving the Son a glorified setting for His sufferings. He must not, He could not fail of that glory. "Who for the joy that was set before Him endured the cross, despising the shame, and is set down at the right hand of the throne of God" (Heb. 12:2).

In portraying the experience of the Son a mighty "wherefore" links the downward pathway of self-renunciation with the resulting upward sweep of incomparable glory, to a name above every name for time and eternity (Phil. 2:5-11). How we are thrilled with the ovation, coming from myriads of throats, giving voice to that divine "wherefore." Listen! "Worthy is the Lamb that was slain to receive power, and riches, and wisdom, and strength, and honour, and glory, and blessing" (read Rev. 5:11-13).

Dear reader, will you so evaluate your afflictions, whatsoever they be, so yield yourself to their purposed "working for you," that your Heavenly Father can put a like "wherefore" between the sufferings and the "eternal weight of glory" He is reserving in Heaven for you? Write Romans 8:28

over every sorrow and trial and disappointment, as His wisely chosen means to the glory of your becoming "conformed to the image of His Son" (v. 29).

Let Peter bring to your heart's vision this long-range view of Suffering:

> "Wherefore gird up the loins of your mind, be sober, and hope to the end for the grace that is to be brought unto you at the revelation of Jesus Christ" (I Pet. 1:13). ". . . a witness of the sufferings of Christ, and also a partaker of the glory that shall be revealed" (I Pet. 5:1).

Scripture even makes the expected experience of glory contingent upon the suffering:

> "If we suffer, we shall also reign with Him" (II Tim. 2:12). "If so be that we suffer with Him, that we may also be glorified together. For I reckon that the sufferings of this present time are not worthy to be compared with the glory which shall be revealed in us" (Rom. 8:17, 18).

Today "we see Jesus, who was made a little lower than the angels for the suffering of death, crowned with glory and honour" (Heb. 2:9); and we hear Him inviting us to go the same road and share the same glory:

> "Fear none of those things which thou shalt suffer . . . ye shall have tribulation . . . be thou faithful unto death and I will give thee the crown of life (Rev. 2:10). "To him that overcometh will I grant to sit with Me in My throne, even as I also overcame and am set down with My Father in His throne" (Rev. 3:21).

Bringing the Glory Down to Earth

Stephen was the first of an honored company, privileged to follow their Lord in the suffering of martyrdom—the supreme witness. And Stephen's Lord honored and encouraged him with a preview of the glory awaiting him. The heavens opened as in readiness to welcome him, and he "saw the glory of God, and Jesus standing"—refusing to remain seated—eager to welcome him to the gloryland (Acts 7:55, 56).

Not only did Stephen see the up-yonder glory so soon to be his; his traducers saw that glory brought down to their vision level: "All that sat in the council, looking steadfastly on him, saw his face as it had been the face of an angel" (Acts 6:15). What a sight for murderers' eyes! God put His glory into the soul of His sufferer, and it shone out upon his face.

Our Lord Jesus brought the Glory of Suffering down to earth, He who had suffered as the Lamb slain from eternity, that men, if they would, might see "the light of the knowledge of the glory of God in the face of Jesus Christ" (II Cor. 4:6).

The time came when our Lord set His face toward the suffering of death. He "began to show unto His disciples how that He must go unto Jerusalem, and suffer many things . . . and be killed, and be raised again the third day" (Matt. 16:21). Most evidently that suffering had entered into His soul; it must as surely have shown upon His face— not merely the pain of it, but the glory of it.

One day, so it is said, He had brought His little company up to the Holy City, and that evening they gathered around a fire, kindled to keep off the night chill. As He talked to them, one of the disciples noticed that the flare cast the Master's silhouette against the city wall, and, reaching for a burnt ember, he traced those precious features in outline. The fire died out, and they retired for the night. The next morning, as people were passing on their way to work, a curious crowd gathered before the strange portrait. There were many conjectures as to who it might be. A cobbler remarked, "He is bent over, just like a cobbler at his bench; it might be one such as I." A fish vendor in the crowd said, "No, don't you see his lips are open; he's hawking his wares, just like me." But a proud Pharisee said, "No, you all are mistaken; don't you see that noble brow. He's one of my class. Why, it might be a picture of me." But a humble by-stander, as he gazed upon that face, felt a strange longing rising in his heart. "Oh," said he, "Oh, that one could be like that!" And, in response to his humble heart-longing, so it is said, the likeness of Christ leaped from the wall to shine out in his face; and men turned from the lifeless Christ to behold Him living —living in the one who longed to be like Him.

Dare we lay aside our pride, our self-complacency, our pleasure in creature comforts, our desire for outward adornment, all that makes us content to appear well with our fellows on the level of human likeness cast this all aside humbly to offer ourselves as channels for the glory of God to shine out through us? This, for blessing to a world so utterly ignorant of Him. Then may our God implant in us an eagerness to "know Him." As Weymouth renders it: "I long to know Christ and the power which is in His resurrection, and to share in His sufferings and die even as He died" (Phil. 3:10)—a death to self and all that makes for earth's transitory glory—"that the life also of Jesus might be made manifest in our body" (II Cor. 4:10). Anything, that we may become the mirror upon earth of the heavenly glory which our blessed Lord left to suffer for us and which we through suffering shall share with Him.

THE RIGHT ROAD HOME

"Is this the right road home, O Lord?
  The clouds are dark and still,
The stony path is hard to tread,
  Each step brings some fresh hill.
I thought the path would brighter grow,
  And that the sun with warmth would glow,
And joyous songs from free hearts flow.
  IS THIS THE RIGHT ROAD HOME?

Yes, child! This very path I trod:
  The clouds were dark for Me,
The stony path was sharp and hard.
  Not sight, but faith, could see
That at the end the sun shone bright,
  Forever, where there is no night,
Where glad hearts rest from earth's fierce fight.
  IT IS THE RIGHT ROAD HOME!"

WRITINGS OF DR. NORMAN B. HARRISON

BOOKLETS

HIS FULLNESS	HIS GOVERNMENT
HIS MOTHERING	HIS JOY
HIS POWER	HIS LOVE
THE GOSPEL OF JOHN	HIS PEACE
FLOURISHING	H-I-S
SUFFERING	BELONGING
HALLOWING THE HOME	POSSESSING
MODERNIZING YOUR LIFE	EXPERIENCING GOD
HIS COMFORT	NEW TESTAMENT LIVING

STUDY AND DEVOTIONAL BOOKS

HIS SALVATION—Romans
HIS VERY OWN—Ephesians
HIS SIDE VS. OUR SIDE—Galatians
HIS LIFE, LOVE AND LIGHT—John
HIS INDWELLING—The Holy Spirit
HIS IN A LIFE OF PRAYER
HIS IN MIND AND HEART LIVING
HIS LOVE, JOY, PEACE

STUDIES IN PROPHECY

HIS SURE RETURN
THE END—Revelation

Available at your local Christian bookstore or from the publishers

HIS International Service

1515 EAST SIXTY SIXTH STREET • MINNEAPOLIS, MINNESOTA 55423

LAKELAND COLOR PRESS
Minneapolis / Brainerd